365 Days
Make Them Count!

The Planner for the New Year

Activinotes

Activinotes

DAILY JOURNALS, PLANNERS, NOTEBOOKS AND OTHER BLANK BOOKS

Time	Activities for Today	DATE
		M T W T F S S

LEARNINGS FOR THE DAY

_____

_____

_____

_____

REMINDERS FOR TOMORROW:

_____

_____

_____

_____

NOTES FOR THE DAY:

_____

_____

_____

_____

_____

_____

_____

_____

QUICK LIST

	to go	contact
◯ _____		
◯ _____		
◯ _____		
◯ _____		
◯ _____		
◯ _____		
◯ _____		
◯ _____		
◯ _____		

Time	Activities for Today	DATE
		M T W T F S S

LEARNINGS FOR THE DAY

REMINDERS FOR TOMORROW:

NOTES FOR THE DAY:

QUICK LIST

to go

contact

Time	Activities for Today	DATE
		M T W T F S S

LEARNINGS FOR THE DAY

REMINDERS FOR TOMORROW:

NOTES FOR THE DAY:

QUICK LIST

	to go	contact

Time	Activities for Today	DATE
		☐ ☐ ☐ ☐ ☐ ☐ ☐
		M T W T F S S

LEARNINGS FOR THE DAY

_____
_____
_____
_____

REMINDERS FOR TOMORROW:

_____
_____
_____
_____

NOTES FOR THE DAY:

_____
_____
_____
_____
_____
_____
_____
_____

QUICK LIST

	to go	**contact**
◯ _____		
◯ _____		
◯ _____		
◯ _____		
◯ _____		
◯ _____		
◯ _____		
◯ _____		
◯ _____		

Time	Activities for Today	DATE
		M T W T F S S

LEARNINGS FOR THE DAY

REMINDERS FOR TOMORROW:

NOTES FOR THE DAY:

QUICK LIST

to go

contact

Time	Activities for Today	DATE
		M T W T F S S

LEARNINGS FOR THE DAY

REMINDERS FOR TOMORROW:

NOTES FOR THE DAY:

QUICK LIST

to go

contact

Time	Activities for Today	DATE
		M T W T F S S

LEARNINGS FOR THE DAY

REMINDERS FOR TOMORROW:

NOTES FOR THE DAY:

QUICK LIST

	to go	**contact**
◯		
◯		
◯		
◯		
◯		
◯		
◯		
◯		
◯		
◯		

Time	Activities for Today	DATE

		M T W T F S S

LEARNINGS FOR THE DAY

REMINDERS FOR TOMORROW:

NOTES FOR THE DAY:

QUICK LIST

to go	contact

Time	Activities for Today	DATE

M T W T F S S

LEARNINGS FOR THE DAY

REMINDERS FOR TOMORROW:

NOTES FOR THE DAY:

QUICK LIST

to go	contact

Time	Activities for Today	DATE
		M T W T F S S

LEARNINGS FOR THE DAY

REMINDERS FOR TOMORROW:

NOTES FOR THE DAY:

QUICK LIST

to go

contact

Time	Activities for Today	DATE
		M T W T F S S

LEARNINGS FOR THE DAY

REMINDERS FOR TOMORROW:

NOTES FOR THE DAY:

QUICK LIST

	to go	contact

Time	Activities for Today	DATE
		M T W T F S S

LEARNINGS FOR THE DAY

REMINDERS FOR TOMORROW:

NOTES FOR THE DAY:

QUICK LIST

to go

contact

Time	Activities for Today	DATE
		M T W T F S S

LEARNINGS FOR THE DAY

REMINDERS FOR TOMORROW:

NOTES FOR THE DAY:

QUICK LIST

to go

contact

Time	Activities for Today	DATE
		M T W T F S S

LEARNINGS FOR THE DAY

REMINDERS FOR TOMORROW:

NOTES FOR THE DAY:

QUICK LIST

to go

contact

Time	Activities for Today	DATE
		M T W T F S S

LEARNINGS FOR THE DAY

REMINDERS FOR TOMORROW:

NOTES FOR THE DAY:

QUICK LIST

to go

contact

Time	Activities for Today	DATE
		M T W T F S S

LEARNINGS FOR THE DAY

REMINDERS FOR TOMORROW:

NOTES FOR THE DAY:

QUICK LIST

to go

contact

Time	Activities for Today	DATE
		M T W T F S S

LEARNINGS FOR THE DAY
_____
_____
_____
_____

REMINDERS FOR TOMORROW:
_____
_____
_____
_____

NOTES FOR THE DAY:
_____
_____
_____
_____
_____
_____
_____
_____

QUICK LIST

	to go	contact

Time	Activities for Today	DATE
		M T W T F S S

LEARNINGS FOR THE DAY

REMINDERS FOR TOMORROW:

NOTES FOR THE DAY:

QUICK LIST

to go

contact

Time	Activities for Today	DATE
		M T W T F S S

LEARNINGS FOR THE DAY

REMINDERS FOR TOMORROW:

NOTES FOR THE DAY:

QUICK LIST

to go

contact

Time	Activities for Today	DATE
		M T W T F S S

LEARNINGS FOR THE DAY

REMINDERS FOR TOMORROW:

NOTES FOR THE DAY:

QUICK LIST

to go

contact

Time	Activities for Today	DATE
		M T W T F S S

LEARNINGS FOR THE DAY

REMINDERS FOR TOMORROW:

NOTES FOR THE DAY:

QUICK LIST

to go

contact

Time	Activities for Today	DATE
		M T W T F S S

LEARNINGS FOR THE DAY

REMINDERS FOR TOMORROW:

NOTES FOR THE DAY:

QUICK LIST

to go

contact.

Time	Activities for Today	DATE
		M T W T F S S

LEARNINGS FOR THE DAY

REMINDERS FOR TOMORROW:

NOTES FOR THE DAY:

QUICK LIST

to go	contact

Time	Activities for Today	DATE
		M T W T F S S

LEARNINGS FOR THE DAY

_____
_____
_____
_____

REMINDERS FOR TOMORROW:

_____
_____
_____
_____

NOTES FOR THE DAY:

_____
_____
_____
_____
_____
_____
_____
_____

QUICK LIST

to go

contact

Time	Activities for Today	DATE
		M T W T F S S

LEARNINGS FOR THE DAY

REMINDERS FOR TOMORROW:

NOTES FOR THE DAY:

QUICK LIST

to go

contact

Time	Activities for Today	DATE
		M T W T F S S

LEARNINGS FOR THE DAY

REMINDERS FOR TOMORROW:

NOTES FOR THE DAY:

QUICK LIST

to go

contact

Time	Activities for Today	DATE
		M T W T F S S

LEARNINGS FOR THE DAY

REMINDERS FOR TOMORROW:

NOTES FOR THE DAY:

QUICK LIST

to go	contact

Time	Activities for Today	DATE
		M T W T F S S

LEARNINGS FOR THE DAY

REMINDERS FOR TOMORROW:

NOTES FOR THE DAY:

QUICK LIST

to go	contact

Time	Activities for Today	DATE
		M T W T F S S

LEARNINGS FOR THE DAY

REMINDERS FOR TOMORROW:

NOTES FOR THE DAY:

QUICK LIST

to go

contact

Time	Activities for Today	DATE
		M T W T F S S

LEARNINGS FOR THE DAY

_____
_____
_____
_____

REMINDERS FOR TOMORROW:

_____
_____
_____
_____

NOTES FOR THE DAY:

_____
_____
_____
_____
_____
_____
_____
_____
_____

QUICK LIST

to go | contact

Time	Activities for Today	DATE
		M T W T F S S

LEARNINGS FOR THE DAY
_____
_____
_____
_____

REMINDERS FOR TOMORROW:
_____
_____
_____
_____

NOTES FOR THE DAY:
_____
_____
_____
_____
_____
_____
_____
_____
_____

QUICK LIST

	to go	contact

Time	Activities for Today	DATE
		M T W T F S S

LEARNINGS FOR THE DAY

REMINDERS FOR TOMORROW:

NOTES FOR THE DAY:

QUICK LIST

to go

contact

Time	Activities for Today	DATE
		M T W T F S S

LEARNINGS FOR THE DAY

REMINDERS FOR TOMORROW:

NOTES FOR THE DAY:

QUICK LIST

to go

contact

Time	Activities for Today	DATE
		M T W T F S S

LEARNINGS FOR THE DAY

REMINDERS FOR TOMORROW:

NOTES FOR THE DAY:

QUICK LIST

to go

contact

Time	Activities for Today	DATE
		M T W T F S S

LEARNINGS FOR THE DAY

REMINDERS FOR TOMORROW:

NOTES FOR THE DAY:

QUICK LIST

to go	contact

Time	Activities for Today	DATE
		M T W T F S S

LEARNINGS FOR THE DAY

REMINDERS FOR TOMORROW:

NOTES FOR THE DAY:

QUICK LIST

to go

contact

Time	Activities for Today	DATE
		M T W T F S S

LEARNINGS FOR THE DAY

REMINDERS FOR TOMORROW:

NOTES FOR THE DAY:

QUICK LIST

to go

contact

Time	Activities for Today	DATE
		M T W T F S S

LEARNINGS FOR THE DAY

REMINDERS FOR TOMORROW:

NOTES FOR THE DAY:

QUICK LIST

to go

contact

Time	Activities for Today	DATE
		M T W T F S S

LEARNINGS FOR THE DAY

REMINDERS FOR TOMORROW:

NOTES FOR THE DAY:

QUICK LIST

to go

contact

Time	Activities for Today	DATE
		□ □ □ □ □ □ □
		M T W T F S S

LEARNINGS FOR THE DAY
_____
_____
_____
_____

REMINDERS FOR TOMORROW:
_____
_____
_____
_____

NOTES FOR THE DAY:
_____
_____
_____
_____
_____
_____
_____
_____
_____

QUICK LIST

	to go	contact

Time	Activities for Today	DATE
		M T W T F S S

LEARNINGS FOR THE DAY

_____
_____
_____
_____

REMINDERS FOR TOMORROW:

_____
_____
_____
_____

NOTES FOR THE DAY:

_____
_____
_____
_____
_____
_____
_____
_____
_____

QUICK LIST

	to go	contact

Time	Activities for Today	DATE
		M T W T F S S

LEARNINGS FOR THE DAY

REMINDERS FOR TOMORROW:

NOTES FOR THE DAY:

QUICK LIST

to go

contact

Time	Activities for Today	DATE
		M T W T F S S

LEARNINGS FOR THE DAY
_____
_____
_____
_____

REMINDERS FOR TOMORROW:
_____
_____
_____
_____

NOTES FOR THE DAY:
_____
_____
_____
_____
_____
_____
_____
_____

QUICK LIST

	to go	**contact**
◯ _____		
◯ _____		
◯ _____		
◯ _____		
◯ _____		
◯ _____		
◯ _____		
◯ _____		
◯ _____		
◯ _____		

Time	Activities for Today	DATE
		M T W T F S S

LEARNINGS FOR THE DAY

REMINDERS FOR TOMORROW:

NOTES FOR THE DAY:

QUICK LIST

to go

contact

Time	Activities for Today	DATE
		M T W T F S S

LEARNINGS FOR THE DAY

REMINDERS FOR TOMORROW:

NOTES FOR THE DAY:

QUICK LIST

to go	contact

Time	Activities for Today	DATE
		M T W T F S S

LEARNINGS FOR THE DAY

REMINDERS FOR TOMORROW:

NOTES FOR THE DAY:

QUICK LIST

to go	contact

Time	Activities for Today	DATE
		M T W T F S S

LEARNINGS FOR THE DAY

REMINDERS FOR TOMORROW:

NOTES FOR THE DAY:

QUICK LIST

to go

contact

Time	Activities for Today	DATE
		M T W T F S S

LEARNINGS FOR THE DAY

REMINDERS FOR TOMORROW:

NOTES FOR THE DAY:

QUICK LIST

to go	contact

Time	Activities for Today	DATE
		M T W T F S S

LEARNINGS FOR THE DAY

REMINDERS FOR TOMORROW:

NOTES FOR THE DAY:

QUICK LIST

to go

contact

Time	Activities for Today	DATE						
		M	T	W	T	F	S	S

LEARNINGS FOR THE DAY

REMINDERS FOR TOMORROW:

NOTES FOR THE DAY:

QUICK LIST

to go

contact

Time	Activities for Today	DATE
		M T W T F S S

LEARNINGS FOR THE DAY

REMINDERS FOR TOMORROW:

NOTES FOR THE DAY:

QUICK LIST

to go

contact

Time	Activities for Today	DATE
		☐ ☐ ☐ ☐ ☐ ☐ ☐
		M T W T F S S

LEARNINGS FOR THE DAY

REMINDERS FOR TOMORROW:

NOTES FOR THE DAY:

QUICK LIST

	to go	contact
◯		
◯		
◯		
◯		
◯		
◯		
◯		
◯		
◯		

Time	Activities for Today	DATE
		M T W T F S S

LEARNINGS FOR THE DAY

REMINDERS FOR TOMORROW:

NOTES FOR THE DAY:

QUICK LIST

to go

contact

Time	Activities for Today	DATE
		M T W T F S S

LEARNINGS FOR THE DAY

_____
_____
_____
_____

REMINDERS FOR TOMORROW:

_____
_____
_____
_____

NOTES FOR THE DAY:

_____
_____
_____
_____
_____
_____
_____
_____
_____
_____

QUICK LIST

	to go	contact
○ _____		
○ _____		
○ _____		
○ _____		
○ _____		
○ _____		
○ _____		
○ _____		
○ _____		
○ _____		

Time	Activities for Today	DATE
		M T W T F S S

LEARNINGS FOR THE DAY

REMINDERS FOR TOMORROW:

NOTES FOR THE DAY:

QUICK LIST

to go

contact

Time	Activities for Today	DATE
		M T W T F S S

LEARNINGS FOR THE DAY

REMINDERS FOR TOMORROW:

NOTES FOR THE DAY:

QUICK LIST

to go	contact

Time	Activities for Today	DATE

M T W T F S S

LEARNINGS FOR THE DAY

REMINDERS FOR TOMORROW:

NOTES FOR THE DAY:

QUICK LIST

to go

contact

Time	Activities for Today	DATE
		M T W T F S S

LEARNINGS FOR THE DAY

REMINDERS FOR TOMORROW:

NOTES FOR THE DAY:

QUICK LIST

to go

contact

Time	Activities for Today	DATE
		M T W T F S S

LEARNINGS FOR THE DAY

REMINDERS FOR TOMORROW:

NOTES FOR THE DAY:

QUICK LIST

to go

contact

Time	Activities for Today	DATE
		M T W T F S S

LEARNINGS FOR THE DAY
_____
_____
_____
_____

REMINDERS FOR TOMORROW:
_____
_____
_____
_____

NOTES FOR THE DAY:
_____
_____
_____
_____
_____
_____
_____
_____
_____

QUICK LIST

	to go	contact
○		
○		
○		
○		
○		
○		
○		
○		
○		

Time	Activities for Today	DATE
		M T W T F S S

LEARNINGS FOR THE DAY

REMINDERS FOR TOMORROW:

NOTES FOR THE DAY:

QUICK LIST

to go

contact

Time	Activities for Today	DATE
		M T W T F S S

LEARNINGS FOR THE DAY

REMINDERS FOR TOMORROW:

NOTES FOR THE DAY:

QUICK LIST

to go

contact

Time	Activities for Today	DATE
		M T W T F S S

LEARNINGS FOR THE DAY

REMINDERS FOR TOMORROW:

NOTES FOR THE DAY:

QUICK LIST

to go

contact

Time	Activities for Today	DATE
		M T W T F S S

LEARNINGS FOR THE DAY

REMINDERS FOR TOMORROW:

NOTES FOR THE DAY:

QUICK LIST

to go	contact

Time	Activities for Today	DATE
		M T W T F S S

LEARNINGS FOR THE DAY

REMINDERS FOR TOMORROW:

NOTES FOR THE DAY:

QUICK LIST

to go	contact

Time	Activities for Today	DATE
		☐ ☐ ☐ ☐ ☐ ☐ ☐
		M T W T F S S

LEARNINGS FOR THE DAY

REMINDERS FOR TOMORROW:

NOTES FOR THE DAY:

QUICK LIST

○ _____
○ _____
○ _____
○ _____
○ _____
○ _____
○ _____
○ _____
○ _____

to go	contact

Time	Activities for Today	DATE
		M T W T F S S

LEARNINGS FOR THE DAY

REMINDERS FOR TOMORROW:

NOTES FOR THE DAY:

QUICK LIST

to go

contact

Time	Activities for Today	DATE
		M T W T F S S

LEARNINGS FOR THE DAY

REMINDERS FOR TOMORROW:

NOTES FOR THE DAY:

QUICK LIST

to go	contact

Time	Activities for Today	DATE
		M T W T F S S

LEARNINGS FOR THE DAY

REMINDERS FOR TOMORROW:

NOTES FOR THE DAY:

QUICK LIST

to go

contact

Time	Activities for Today	DATE
		☐ ☐ ☐ ☐ ☐ ☐ ☐
		M T W T F S S

LEARNINGS FOR THE DAY

_____
_____
_____
_____

REMINDERS FOR TOMORROW:

_____
_____
_____
_____

NOTES FOR THE DAY:

_____
_____
_____
_____
_____
_____
_____
_____
_____

QUICK LIST

	to go	contact
◯ _____		
◯ _____		
◯ _____		
◯ _____		
◯ _____		
◯ _____		
◯ _____		
◯ _____		
◯ _____		

Time	Activities for Today	DATE
		M T W T F S S

LEARNINGS FOR THE DAY

REMINDERS FOR TOMORROW:

NOTES FOR THE DAY:

QUICK LIST

to go

contact

Time	Activities for Today	DATE
		M T W T F S S

LEARNINGS FOR THE DAY

REMINDERS FOR TOMORROW:

NOTES FOR THE DAY:

QUICK LIST

to go	contact

Time	Activities for Today	DATE
		M T W T F S S

LEARNINGS FOR THE DAY

_____
_____
_____
_____

REMINDERS FOR TOMORROW:

_____
_____
_____
_____

NOTES FOR THE DAY:

_____
_____
_____
_____
_____
_____
_____
_____
_____

QUICK LIST

	to go	**contact**
◯ _____		
◯ _____		
◯ _____		
◯ _____		
◯ _____		
◯ _____		
◯ _____		
◯ _____		
◯ _____		
◯ _____		

Time	Activities for Today	DATE
		M T W T F S S

LEARNINGS FOR THE DAY

REMINDERS FOR TOMORROW:

NOTES FOR THE DAY:

QUICK LIST

to go	contact

Time	Activities for Today	DATE
		M T W T F S S

LEARNINGS FOR THE DAY

REMINDERS FOR TOMORROW:

NOTES FOR THE DAY:

QUICK LIST

to go

contact

Time	Activities for Today	DATE
		M T W T F S S

LEARNINGS FOR THE DAY

REMINDERS FOR TOMORROW:

NOTES FOR THE DAY:

QUICK LIST

to go	contact

Time	Activities for Today	DATE
		M T W T F S S

LEARNINGS FOR THE DAY

REMINDERS FOR TOMORROW:

NOTES FOR THE DAY:

QUICK LIST

to go

contact

Time	Activities for Today	DATE
		M T W T F S S

LEARNINGS FOR THE DAY
_____
_____
_____
_____

REMINDERS FOR TOMORROW:
_____
_____
_____
_____

NOTES FOR THE DAY:
_____
_____
_____
_____
_____
_____
_____
_____
_____

QUICK LIST

to go

contact

Time	Activities for Today	DATE
		M T W T F S S

LEARNINGS FOR THE DAY

REMINDERS FOR TOMORROW:

NOTES FOR THE DAY:

QUICK LIST

to go	contact

Time	Activities for Today	DATE
		M T W T F S S

LEARNINGS FOR THE DAY

_____
_____
_____
_____

REMINDERS FOR TOMORROW:

_____
_____
_____
_____

NOTES FOR THE DAY:

_____
_____
_____
_____
_____
_____
_____
_____
_____
_____

QUICK LIST

○ _____
○ _____
○ _____
○ _____
○ _____
○ _____
○ _____
○ _____
○ _____
○ _____

to go

contact

Time	Activities for Today	DATE
		M T W T F S S

LEARNINGS FOR THE DAY

REMINDERS FOR TOMORROW:

NOTES FOR THE DAY:

QUICK LIST

to go	contact

Time	Activities for Today	DATE
		M T W T F S S

LEARNINGS FOR THE DAY

REMINDERS FOR TOMORROW:

NOTES FOR THE DAY:

QUICK LIST

to go	contact

Time	Activities for Today	DATE
		M T W T F S S

LEARNINGS FOR THE DAY

REMINDERS FOR TOMORROW:

NOTES FOR THE DAY:

QUICK LIST

to go

contact

Time	Activities for Today	DATE
		☐ ☐ ☐ ☐ ☐ ☐
		M T W T F S S

LEARNINGS FOR THE DAY

_____
_____
_____
_____

REMINDERS FOR TOMORROW:

_____
_____
_____
_____

NOTES FOR THE DAY:

_____
_____
_____
_____
_____
_____
_____
_____
_____

QUICK LIST

	to go	contact
◯ _____		
◯ _____		
◯ _____		
◯ _____		
◯ _____		
◯ _____		
◯ _____		
◯ _____		
◯ _____		
◯ _____		

Time	Activities for Today	DATE
		M T W T F S S

LEARNINGS FOR THE DAY

REMINDERS FOR TOMORROW:

NOTES FOR THE DAY:

QUICK LIST

to go	contact

Time	Activities for Today	DATE
		M T W T F S S

LEARNINGS FOR THE DAY

REMINDERS FOR TOMORROW:

NOTES FOR THE DAY:

QUICK LIST

to go

contact

Time	Activities for Today	DATE
		M T W T F S S

LEARNINGS FOR THE DAY

REMINDERS FOR TOMORROW:

NOTES FOR THE DAY:

QUICK LIST

to go	contact

Time	Activities for Today	DATE
		M T W T F S S

LEARNINGS FOR THE DAY

REMINDERS FOR TOMORROW:

NOTES FOR THE DAY:

QUICK LIST

to go

contact

Time	Activities for Today	DATE
		M T W T F S S

LEARNINGS FOR THE DAY
_____
_____
_____
_____

REMINDERS FOR TOMORROW:
_____
_____
_____
_____

NOTES FOR THE DAY:
_____
_____
_____
_____
_____
_____
_____
_____
_____

QUICK LIST

	to go	contact

Time	Activities for Today	DATE
		M T W T F S S

LEARNINGS FOR THE DAY

REMINDERS FOR TOMORROW:

NOTES FOR THE DAY:

QUICK LIST

to go

contact

Time	Activities for Today	DATE
		M T W T F S S

LEARNINGS FOR THE DAY

REMINDERS FOR TOMORROW:

NOTES FOR THE DAY:

QUICK LIST

to go	contact

Time	Activities for Today	DATE
		M T W T F S S

LEARNINGS FOR THE DAY

REMINDERS FOR TOMORROW:

NOTES FOR THE DAY:

QUICK LIST

○

○

○

○

○

○

○

○

○

○

to go

contact

Time	Activities for Today	DATE
		M T W T F S S

LEARNINGS FOR THE DAY

REMINDERS FOR TOMORROW:

NOTES FOR THE DAY:

QUICK LIST

to go

contact

Time	Activities for Today	DATE
		M T W T F S S

LEARNINGS FOR THE DAY

REMINDERS FOR TOMORROW:

NOTES FOR THE DAY:

QUICK LIST

to go

contact

Time	Activities for Today	DATE
		M T W T F S S

LEARNINGS FOR THE DAY

REMINDERS FOR TOMORROW:

NOTES FOR THE DAY:

QUICK LIST

to go

contact

Time	Activities for Today	DATE
		M T W T F S S

LEARNINGS FOR THE DAY

REMINDERS FOR TOMORROW:

NOTES FOR THE DAY:

QUICK LIST

to go

contact

Time	Activities for Today	DATE
		☐☐☐☐☐☐☐
		M T W T F S S

LEARNINGS FOR THE DAY

REMINDERS FOR TOMORROW:

NOTES FOR THE DAY:

QUICK LIST

to go

contact

Time	Activities for Today	DATE
		☐ ☐ ☐ ☐ ☐ ☐ ☐
		M T W T F S S

LEARNINGS FOR THE DAY

_____
_____
_____
_____

REMINDERS FOR TOMORROW:

_____
_____
_____
_____

NOTES FOR THE DAY:

_____
_____
_____
_____
_____
_____
_____
_____
_____

QUICK LIST

○ _____
○ _____
○ _____
○ _____
○ _____
○ _____
○ _____
○ _____
○ _____

to go

contact

Time	Activities for Today	DATE
		M T W T F S S

LEARNINGS FOR THE DAY

REMINDERS FOR TOMORROW:

NOTES FOR THE DAY:

QUICK LIST

to go

contact

Time	Activities for Today	DATE
		M T W T F S S

LEARNINGS FOR THE DAY

REMINDERS FOR TOMORROW:

NOTES FOR THE DAY:

QUICK LIST

to go

contact

Time	Activities for Today	DATE
		M T W T F S S

LEARNINGS FOR THE DAY

REMINDERS FOR TOMORROW:

NOTES FOR THE DAY:

QUICK LIST

to go

contact

Time	Activities for Today	DATE
		M T W T F S S

LEARNINGS FOR THE DAY

REMINDERS FOR TOMORROW:

NOTES FOR THE DAY:

QUICK LIST

to go	contact

Time	Activities for Today	DATE
		M T W T F S S

LEARNINGS FOR THE DAY

_____
_____
_____
_____

REMINDERS FOR TOMORROW:

_____
_____
_____
_____

NOTES FOR THE DAY:

_____
_____
_____
_____
_____
_____
_____
_____
_____

QUICK LIST

○ _____
○ _____
○ _____
○ _____
○ _____
○ _____
○ _____
○ _____
○ _____
○ _____

to go	contact

Time	Activities for Today	DATE
		M T W T F S S

LEARNINGS FOR THE DAY

REMINDERS FOR TOMORROW:

NOTES FOR THE DAY:

QUICK LIST

to go	contact